Contents

Introduction

A prayer meeting is about to begin. As people enter the high school gymnasium, a smiling girl distributing name tags pauses to greet one man who obviously feels out of place. They spend a few minutes talking before he rejoins the crowd. More than 500 people—young, old, men, women, students, housewives, businessmen—are enthusiastically gathering in concentric rows of folding chairs. In the center, a group of guitarists begins to play. "Sing to God a brand new, brand new canticle ..." The handshaking and hugging ends as everyone finds a chair and a songbook; the lively song begins to pick up momentum "... and let the nations shout and clap their hands for joy." Tonight there is special enthusiasm. It is Easter week. When the song ends, the prayer meeting leader is already standing in the middle. "Let the nations shout and clap for joy," he says, picking up the refrain of the song. "It is with great joy we remember that Jesus died and has risen. And with great joy we gather to acknowledge his salvation. We are gathered as a community in prayer... Let us respond to the Lord with joyful praise."

Immediately there is a burst of spontaneous prayer from all sides. Nearly everyone is praying out loud. Out of the rising murmur of prayer come phrases, "Praise to you ... halleluia ... hosanna ... you are the life, Jesus." Off to one side, someone begins to sing a free-flowing melody. The song is quickly picked up, sweeping over the meeting mingled with the spoken words which fade before the gathering swell of praise. Not one, but hundreds of songs weave together in harmony. Someone begins to clap slowly, then stops as the music fades and disappears, yielding to a chorus of song. "Holy, holy, holy Lord, God of hosts, heaven and earth are filled with your glory ..." Some hands are lifted, most faces upturned, eyes closed. Within five minutes the previously bustling crowd is deep in prayer.

"O risen Lord, all praise to you," a voice prays aloud. The murmur of prayer continues from all directions until it is silenced by a strong voice speaking aloud a message in tongues. For a half-minute it is so quiet one can hear his own breathing. Then, the awaited interpretation comes from another part of the room, "My children, I call you tonight ... Hear my voice in your hearts now ... I claim each of you as my child.... Answer me with your hearts open to my love."

The ongoing murmuring words of prayer resume, more subdued, meditative, responding to the word just spoken. Things are building. A man's voice intones, "My soul doth magnify the Lord. . . ," and the song is picked up. Clapping steadily grows. The harmonies increase as the song builds and is repeated until, dying out, it is again replaced by the everpresent words of prayer. Shortly, a prophecy is spoken boldly and with confidence by a woman who is obviously experienced in prophesying, "Listen to me all you who seek me with your whole heart. You will not be let down by me. . . I will not let you down. . . Yes, I am among you and have overcome death and sin. I have a full life for you. . . Look to me now." The murmuring prayer that follows is louder, enthusiastic, thankful. Another prophesy follows, "Rejoice, lift up your hands and your hearts and rejoice." A new voice raises a song loudly, brightly, with clapping and tambourine, "Glory to God, glory! O praise him alleluia!"

Minutes later the leader says, "Let's stand and thank the Lord for his resurrection and for giving us his joy." The rumble and rattle of the crowd rising to its feet is quickly drowned in the loud praise that rushes up quickly into singing, the same free-flowing singing in the Spirit with which the meeting began, now stronger and sustained.

The meeting continues. Always there is the flowing murmur of prayer interspersed with song, prophecy, and then, increasingly, brief exhortations to seek the Lord, to thank the Lord, to live for the Lord. One man enjoins us with a brief exposition of John, chapter three, to respond to the call of the Lord with all our hearts.

Later, the leader introduces a man from among the group who speaks for twenty minutes about the resurrection of Jesus and the promise of resurrection which it holds for us. His teaching is well-prepared, but clearly energized by the Spirit at work in the meeting. Some things strike us funny and everyone readily laughs, while the word itself is taken seriously. When he sits down, the spontaneous prayer is more vigorous than before.

On the edge of the crowd a young man starts speaking about a passage from Scripture. He is hard to hear and after a few minutes the meeting is restless but patient. When he finishes there is some uncertain quiet prayer, the direction of the meeting seems unclear. People are waiting.

The leader rises and introduces a second man who will share "what God has been doing in his life." He is a young man with a family, working as a journalist. He describes in straightforward terms his own journey from cynicism and disbelief to faith. His style is light and everyone laughs freely, but the message hits home.

Shortly after, the meeting ends. We stand again to sing several lively songs. Most people put their arms around others and sway in time with the music. Two hours never seemed to have gone so quickly.

4

Daily around the world this scene is repeated in the central meeting and chief instrument of the charismatic renewal—the prayer meeting. In large community gatherings like the one described above, or in home groupings, at regional days of renewal, or international conferences, the prayer meeting draws together young and old in prayer and worship. From the very beginning of the charismatic movement, the prayer meeting has been spontaneously adopted as the natural expression of the movement. In the words of one writer, "It has proved to be an ideal vehicle to such an extent that wherever the movement has spread, the prayer meetings have gone with it. It is almost impossible to visualize it without them."[1]

As we grow in our personal relationship with the Lord, we usually seek guidance from other Christians on how to pray and worship the Lord. Likewise, as a group of Christians worshipping together, we can seek guidance and learn how to yield to *all* the Spirit of God has for us as a body.

This booklet discusses the dynamics of prayer meetings, offering insight into four major areas: worship, hearing the Lord's word, order, and evangelism at prayer meetings. The guidelines offered are not intended primarily for leaders of prayer meetings, although it will be helpful and informative for leaders. Rather, it is for every person who attends a prayer meeting, whether it

---

[1] O'Connor, Edward, C.S.C. *The Pentecostal Movement in the Catholic Church.* Notre Dame, Indiana (Ave Maria), p.112.

is a home group of ten people or a weekly gathering of hundreds. Every Christian needs to listen to the Spirit and grow in greater freedom and depth in praising the Lord.

CHAPTER ONE

Worship

> "... We are gathered as a community in prayer. Let us respond to the Lord with joyful praise."
>
> Immediately there is a burst of spontaneous prayer from all sides. Nearly everyone is praying out loud.

It is difficult to adequately verbalize the experience of worshipping God, but it can be readily experienced in a prayer meeting. Worship means an explicit turning to God. Our prayer meetings must be God-centered if they are to be worshipful; **we** must have that profound sense that we are gathered not just for ourselves, but for God. We must look to God, recall his nearness, and yield our hearts to his movement. If we allow our minds to wander, we will find it difficult to worship. The prayer meeting is a time to put aside other concerns and to think of God himself; it gives us the chance to do something that we almost never do—turning aside from other concerns, looking to God himself, and then expressing in word and song our appreciation of his greatness, power, love, and might.

Like many others, I had never been able to make much sense of the concept of worship. It was not that the idea was an unfamiliar one: as a child I had learned that worship was the purpose of the services at church. When I first seriously committed my life to Jesus, I was told that worship and adoration were the most important forms of prayer. Yet Sunday services and my personal prayer seldom seemed to express worship.

Some told me that worship was accomplished by regular attendance at church, by faithfulness to meditative prayer, or charity in daily life, and was not a unique identifiable experience. Others felt that the notion of worship should be abandoned altogether.

When I was first baptized in the Spirit and began to experience prayer in tongues, I had a very distinct sense that the prayer, unintelligible to me, was an act of praise. It was the first time that I had experienced what it was like to worship God. Not very many weeks after I found myself reflecting, "Somehow I feel that for the first time I am doing what I was created to do. I feel like the round peg that just got placed in the round hole." I do not imagine that anyone could previously have explained to me the centrality of worship. But when I experienced it, almost no explanation was needed. As the Scriptures say, we indeed have been formed to *"live for the praise of his glory"* (Eph. 1:12).

When the leader of a prayer meeting says "Let's worship the Lord," we know that he is speaking about something very definite, something different from the dozens of other activities that make up our Christian life. He is talking about a conscious turning to God and expressing in word and song a heartfelt awe, reverence, thanksgiving, and praise—a love of God for his own sake.

Worship during a prayer meeting should be predominant. We are so unused to worship that many cannot continue it for more than a few minutes without feeling "Okay, now let's *do* something." But worship *is* something. It ought to be seen as the purpose of the prayer meeting, and not a preliminary exercise to get started. It is a concrete way that we can respond to the words of Jesus: "This is the first and greatest commandment: that you shall love the Lord your God with all your mind and all your heart and all your strength." Psalm 150 says:

"Praise the Lord
Praise God in his sanctuary. . .
Praise him for his mighty deeds. . .
Let everything that breathes praise the Lord."

We should always be aware that this, the joyous praise of the Lord, is at the heart of the prayer meeting. But, in addition to hearts that are turned to the Lord, there are several other elements that are involved in this worship. Without losing sight of the central purpose of the prayer meeting, I would like to elaborate on the various elements that contribute to worship and praise.

Word of Prayer

I suppose I shall never forget the evening that the first group from Notre Dame to be baptized in the Spirit met in the home of Ray Bullard, the president of the local chapter of The Full Gospel Businessmen's Fellowship. Ray had gathered about twenty men from the area to meet with the new group of Catholic pentecostals that had called and asked to pray together with him and a few friends. We unsuspectingly entered Ray's basement and found ourselves surrounded. Once we were all comfortably settled Ray said, "Well, let's begin with a word of prayer." What a shock to us when suddenly everyone in the room simultaneously burst into loud and enthusiastic prayer. I was accustomed to spontaneous prayer but nothing like this. I was about ready to say, "Wait a minute, I can't tell what you're saying." So strange did this kind of prayer seem to us (along with the many other strange things we were to hear that night) that one of those present later remarked, "If this charismatic renewal were merely a human fiction, or even a form of religiosity created out of the wills of men, I really believe it would have crumbled to dust that evening." Far from crumbling to dust, God's Spirit taught us many things about prayer. That evening we began to learn how to join in a "word of prayer."

The word of prayer, unusual as it may seem, has become a hallmark of the charismatic prayer meeting for good reason. This kind of prayer enables a group to pray together in an active, participative way that builds a spirit of unity and praise. If in our meetings we were to pray only silently when we pray as a group, or only used recited prayers, we would be greatly impoverished. When the leader says, "Let's all pray together," how natural it seems that we should do so vocally, in a way that demonstrates the reality of our prayer.

In the word of prayer the object is not to share a prayer with others so that they can understand our prayer and join with it in their minds. Rather, the word of prayer allows for a form of group personal prayer. Each of us prays individually to God in our own words or in tongues, praying aloud in a moderate tone of voice (generally), so that others can hear that we are praying and be built up and encouraged to pray more fervently themselves. In this form of prayer no single voice is supposed to dominate. Rather, the voices ought to blend together in volume so that one's individual prayer becomes part of the whole prayer of the community.

The word of prayer should not be allowed to become mechanical. Each one ought to sincerely intend the prayer that he makes. One must bear in mind that the measure of the sincerity of our prayer is not emotion or feeling, it is intention. Even on occasions when one finds it difficult to pray or finds himself unenthusiastic about praying he can pray sincerely, meaning the words of the prayer, and keeping before his eyes the purpose of worship—it is for God, not for us.

Shared Prayer

Shared prayer, as the name implies, is the prayer of one person made aloud while others listen and join themselves to the prayer. A priest offering the collect at Mass or a minister speaking out a prayer at the Sunday service, is offering a shared prayer. In meetings, shared prayer is usually spontaneous. The Holy Spirit frequently inspires shared prayer, and it can have a powerful effect upon the whole meeting. A psalm when read sincerely as a prayer can effectively build the worship of the meeting, too. The Holy Spirit provides appropriate occasions for shared prayer. A period of silence or quiet prayer together is usually the most opportune time. When everyone is praying together at any volume, trying to shout over the word of prayer does not contribute to the peace or sense of order in the meeting. We can wait, for the Spirit will give the opening.

In our meetings in the last year there has developed a form of shared prayer that has been especially effective as an instrument of worship. Frequently people will begin to praise the Lord in a series of short acclamations. "You are the creator," one will say. "We praise you, the Lord of glory," another will pray. And then another, "Jesus, you are the good shepherd." Sometimes

12

these acclamations of praise will come one after another for several minutes, resulting in a beautiful litany of praise.

Silent Prayer

There are times too in a prayer meeting when silence is indeed a way of worship. Often, after a period of vigorous praise and song, there will suddenly be a strong silence in which one feels the presence and holiness of God. Such a silence is alive, so different from the dead silence of lifeless worship. At such moments, silence is the expression of our awe and reverence for God's holiness and is as filled with the presence of the Spirit as singing in tongues. There will be such special moments in a prayer meeting and we should not be afraid of them, but silence does not seem to be the primary mode of participation in the prayer meeting. The prayer meeting is not really for group meditation in silence nor for personal prayer. The prayer meeting's genius is precisely in its participative and expressive character.

Singing

Singing is one of the most effective means of expressing community worship. Our meetings invariably begin with song, and for good reason: music and song immediately unite us in prayer, lifting our spirits and opening us to the working of God.

Many of us have experienced moments in our prayer meetings when the singing was unified as one voice and the Spirit of the Lord was so powerfully present that we were overwhelmed. We have experienced it perhaps with a song or during a time of singing in tongues. But when we have worshipped the Lord with unity of Spirit and oneness of voice, something has happened and the Holy Spirit has worked deep within us.

Singing with one spirit means yielding to the Holy Spirit in our singing of a song. The main emphasis is on turning to the Lord in song rather than on producing musical excellence. If the Holy Spirit is to form us as he works in each particular song, we must be sensitive to the spirit of the song. Some songs are quiet and worshipful; others are lively and exciting. We should yield to the Spirit of joy, peace, worship, or praise which is appropriate to that song.

Singing can be so much fun that we sometimes get carried away with it. Music can get in the way of what the Lord is doing. Often, a song intrudes on the period of quiet reflection after a prophecy, teaching or exhortation. We sometimes tend to become uncomfortable with any lull in the prayer meeting. We should be wary of this tendency, for moments of silence are frequently from the Lord.

Singing with one Spirit also means singing in a spirit of love for our brothers. St. Paul says in Romans 15:1-2:

We who are strong ought to bear with the failings of the weak, and not to please ourselves; let each of us please his neighbor for his good, to edify him.

This ought to be true in our singing too. Many people, especially those with good voices, often sing as loud as they can to hear themselves. But singing in unity means our voices should be united to the one voice of the body. Our voice should blend with the voices of our brothers. Our ear should be attuned, not to our own voice to see how we are doing, but to the one voice which the Lord is forming among our brothers and sisters. If you are singing so loud that you can hear yourself, you are probably singing too loud. Remember that we are not singing to please ourselves.

On the other hand, singing in unity may mean that some people should sing louder. Many people are afraid to sing at all because they feel that they do not have a good voice or are afraid that they might not be on pitch. For those afraid to sing, love means dying to our fears and lifting our voice in song. If we are attuned to the one voice the Lord is forming in the group, the Lord will join our poor voice to it. I have met many people who thought they could not sing until they began to sing to the Lord in their prayer meetings. Many of these people not only sing, but even start songs. Some people I know say they still cannot sing at all except at a prayer meeting. Then, something happens. The Lord gives them the ability to sing far beyond their natural talent.

The music of a prayer group or community begins to be formed in the proper selection of the songs. When we first heard some of the traditional Pentecostal choruses, we could not imagine ourselves singing such songs. But we have since discovered what a valuable help such choruses are. Their simplicity seems especially suited to the periods of worship in a prayer meeting. Anyone can start them, and everyone can learn them. To this repertoire of choruses, most groups have added many other songs of worship, usually putting together a songsheet so that everyone can sing. If the songsheet is to be used mainly at prayer meetings, only songs appropriate for prayer meetings, especially songs of worship or praise, should be included.

One frequent problem, however, with the music of the pentecostal movement is sentimentality. Sentimental songs, those which express excessive or even false emotion, do not support an emotionally healthy relationship with the Lord. They also frequently "turn off" new people who come to a prayer meeting, especially men. Sentimentality often depends on the manner of singing. Some groups sing a song in a healthy, genuine way while another group will distort the song so that it emerges as excessively sentimental. To avoid sentimentality, remain faithful to the spirit of the song.

Other songs are simply weak or empty from a spiritual point of view. Many songs commonly sung in religious settings have trite or meaningless lyrics. Others have confused and unsingable melodies. Some songs are not explicitly Christian. Such songs simply do not support the prayer of the community; they leave the community feeling distracted or aimless. We can thank the Lord for bringing so much strong and expressive music in the charismatic renewal. We can continue to expect him to provide the kind of songs we need.

Singing in the Spirit

Singing in the Spirit is one of the most beautiful ways of worshipping the Lord. In this kind of prayer each person sings to the Lord in tongues (or English) and in a free melody as the Holy Spirit leads him. The many songs blend together in beautiful harmony. Sometimes the singing in the Spirit can be very soft and peaceful, but at other times very loud and powerful. Singing in the Spirit should be begun when we feel the Lord leading us, rather than just when we feel inclined to. Because it is part of the worship of the meeting, we can count on the Holy Spirit to lead us to begin at the appropriate times.

When the singing in the Spirit begins, each one should hesitate a moment before joining in. Each should look to the Lord and yield his own spirit to the one Holy Spirit to lead him into the song. Each voice should blend with the other voices. (It happens naturally when each one is looking to the Lord and listening to the song which the Spirit is forming.) We can begin to sing softly, letting the Spirit blend us with the song of the community. But we must also step out in faith when singing in the Spirit, having the courage to trust that God will help us, and begin to sing with the expectation that God will form our song. Singing in the Spirit is a high point of expressive worship. It brings us all together to respond actively to the Lord in a way that unites us. In fact, it is something of a barometer of the unity in a prayer meeting—the greater the unity, the more harmonious and unified the singing in the Spirit.

Whether in silence or singing, praying aloud or singing in tongues, the most important thing we should remember is that we are worshipping the Lord. We are keeping our minds and hearts on him. He is worthy of our praise!

"Praise him for his mighty deeds; praise him according to his exceeding greatness! Let everything that breathes praise the Lord!" (Psalm 150)

CHAPTER TWO

God's Word

The meeting continues. Always the flowing murmur of prayer interspersed with song, prophecy, and then, increasingly, brief exhortations to seek the Lord, to thank the Lord, to live for the Lord. One man enjoins us with a brief exposition of John, chapter three, to respond to the call of the Lord with all our hearts.

One of the most unique aspects of our life together as a body of Christians is that God speaks to us. He speaks to us in a way that we can understand and recognize as his voice. Not only does the Spirit draw us into praise of God, he brings forth the word of the Lord through the spiritual gifts, through teaching, and through sharing and exhortation.

In I Corinthians 14:26, Paul says, *"When you come together, each one has a hymn, a lesson, a revelation, a tongue, or an interpretation. Let all things be done for edification."* God wants to speak not only through the recognized leaders and teachers in our prayer meetings, but through the entire community of believers. The leaders have a special responsibility to see that all things are done in order, and to present more developed, prepared teaching, but all of us have a part in speaking the word of the Lord, whether by responding to the Spirit in prophecy or sharing from our own experience.

The two most common means the Lord uses to speak to us in prayer meetings are the spiritual gifts, especially the word gifts of prophecy and tongues with interpretation, and sharing, which includes personal testimony, exhortation, and teaching.

Spiritual Gifts

One area of needed growth in many groups is simply the initial experience of the spiritual gifts. There are still many prayer meetings throughout the world that aspire to be charismatic but find spiritual gifts still lacking. There are some specific steps we can take to find new growth in these areas.

Desire the spiritual gifts. Paul wrote to the Corinthians, *Make love your aim and earnestly desire the spiritual gifts, especially that you may prophesy"* (I Cor. 14:1). This is a startling point. If a prayer group, in unity of heart, desires the spiritual gifts, the Lord will be free to give them. One real problem that many groups face is that the attitude towards spiritual gifts is mixed. Though many would like to see the spiritual gifts present, there are others in the same group who are not so sure. The hesitation and doubt of some communicates itself and tends to make others in the group more hesitant to manifest the spiritual gifts.

This problem should be addressed in teaching by the leaders of the group. It can further be addressed in prayer. If the whole prayer group begins to pray regularly for the spiritual gifts, it will develop a unity in its desire for these gifts which will do much to remove the restraints of fear and mistrust. It must be expressed openly that the prayer group does desire to be charismatic and to experience the gifts of the Spirit. It will be a great help to have expressed to one another their desire for the spiritual gifts and their realization that they might make mistakes. If everyone understands that, and expresses the desire to learn and to support one another during this learning, the individuals will feel much freer to give that first prophecy or message in tongues. It makes a big difference when you know that there is love in the group, that everyone wants to learn about the gifts of the Spirit, and that everyone is going to work together.

Become freer in worship and praise of the Lord. Early in our experience with prayer meetings we learned that the spiritual gifts flow best from a community which has been praising the Lord. We noticed that when there had been little praise the gifts of the Spirit were lacking, weak, or off-center. When the spiritual gifts flow from the heart of a community at worship, they are coming from an atmosphere of unity and centeredness upon the Lord. God alone can give the gifts of the Spirit. If we desire them, let us turn to the Lord himself in praise, and we will be in the best possible position to receive the gifts of the Spirit.

Seek the Lord for his word to us. One great obstacle to the gifts of the Spirit can come from simply not giving the Lord a chance to "get a word in edgewise." Our meetings can be so full of singing, sharing, and reading Scripture passages that little room remains to listen to the Lord. Let there be times when the group agrees to simply wait in prayer for the Lord to speak. During such times, we agree to refrain from sharing just whatever comes to our minds, but wait for the Lord to give us something. For many it can be a fearful thing to "wait on the Lord." We are not accustomed to surrendering our ideas and impulses to him, and we feel awkward when we try to set aside, for even a few minutes, the incessant flow of our own ideas and wait for the Lord to form some word for us.

Have faith that the Lord will give us the gifts of the Spirit. Jesus told us that if we asked anything in his name, the Father would give it to us. We know that the Lord desires that we have the gifts of the Spirit. He has spoken to us through the letters of Paul, saying that we should not be ignorant of the spiritual gifts (I Cor. 12:1) and that the Spirit gives us each a gift for the common good (I Cor. 12:7). We can be confident that the Lord wants to give to our group the gifts of the Spirit. Note that this is different from being confident that the Lord wants to give one particular person all the spiritual gifts. It is the Holy Spirit who distributes the gifts to each *"individually as he wills"* (I Cor. 12:11). The gifts are given to the Body of Christ and it is in the body that we can expect to see the gifts. Because of the needs of the body, we can expect to see the Lord bestow the gifts of the Spirit.

Further, the members of the prayer group need faith to step out and begin to prophesy or give a message in tongues. It is difficult at first for everyone, and requires faith and trust that the Lord will help, and that if we make a mistake, the Lord will prevent its harming others and will teach us how to do better. Paul writes in Romans 12:6 that he who prophesies should prophesy according to his faith. It does take faith to prophesy. No one can come to some point where he no longer needs to have faith in the Lord for manifesting a particular spiritual gift.

Prophecy

When should a person prophesy, speak a message in tongues, or give its interpretation? One important sign is the 'anointing of the Spirit.' An anointing can be described as a quickening of the Spirit—a sense of urgency or expectancy that grows up inside a person. It is a sense of being urged by God to do something or sometimes a feeling of expectancy that God is about to act. The anointing can often affect a person physically; one feels very restless or begins to breathe heavily or feel his heart beat quickly. Jeremiah once described the effect of the Lord anointing him to speak prophetically as like "a fire within my breast"; it is not uncommon that one who begins to prophesy will experience the urging of the Lord in some powerful ways.

Along with the anointing to prophesy, the Holy Spirit gives to the prophet a message. This may come in the form of a few words with which to begin speaking, a general sense of the import of the message, or even a clear idea of the wording of the whole message. When, as generally happens, one experiences an anointing, he should first simply turn to the Lord and seek the Lord himself, and not begin worrying about what to say or try to come up with something. Rather, in the posture of looking to the Lord, he will be able to hear what the Lord has to say.

Being anointed by the Lord does not necessarily mean that one should prophesy. An anointing is an indication, not a compulsion. Many will experience an anointing of the Lord when someone else is going to prophesy. So when one feels that the Lord may be leading him to prophesy, he should ask the Lord for direction. Usually, if one is supposed to prophesy, there is a sense of peace from the Lord indicating that it is right to speak. Then one should wait for an appropriate time to prophesy. For example, it would not be right to interrupt another person speaking. If one receives a word to speak early in the prayer meeting, it may or may not be intended for the beginning moments of the meeting. Generally the Lord's word is better heard when the community has first had an opportunity to praise the Lord and let their minds and hearts become more focused on him. In any case, if one asks the Lord to give him the appropriate time to speak, the Lord will lead him, and over a period of time he will learn to recognize the timing of the Lord.

Administering the word of prophecy or interpretation is very important to its effectiveness. The prophet should speak loudly enough for all to hear, but not so loud as to frighten everyone. He should speak the word in a way that is appropriate to God (St. Peter says, *"Whoever speaks, as one who utters oracles from God"* in 1 Peter 4:11). Also, a prophetic word should be in ordinary English. We would not imagine that if the Lord himself appeared in one of our meetings he would speak to us in Elizabethan English; we would expect him to speak our language, and we expect the same of prophecy.

Most of what is said about giving a prophecy applies to giving a message in tongues. When someone has spoken a message in tongues intended for the whole group to hear, we should all wait in silent prayer until the interpretation is given. The interpretation of such a message in tongues seems to take two forms: sometimes the interpretation is a message like an ordinary prophecy, sometimes it is an inspired prayer like the Psalms.

When a strong prophetic word has been spoken in a meeting, it can have a powerful effect. St.

Paul writes that when one prophesies, he speaks to men for *"their upbuilding and encouragement, and consolation"* (1 Cor. 14:3). This gives us some of the guidelines for testing prophecy. For prophecy is not perfect and so we must weigh what is said (1 Cor. 14:29) and respond to what is of the Lord.

Weighing or testing prophecy is not always easy. There are some objective tests that we have, but just as important is the spiritual discernment of the community. The objective tests are that prophecy should be consistent with Scripture and with sound Christian teaching. The Holy Spirit is not going to speak a word that contradicts in meaning or spirit the revelation that he has already given. Furthermore, prophecy will be consistent with the spirit and character of Jesus. For example, Jesus did not condemn his disciples when he corrected them and neither will the Holy Spirit in prophecy. In addition to these objective tests, a very important test comes through the discernment of the community.

If something is from the Holy Spirit, then those who are living in the Holy Spirit will recognize it. They will feel peace about it and a conviction that it is from the Lord. In a given instance of prophecy there may not be complete unanimity (especially if the prophet is new in the gift), but there will be a general consensus that this is a word from the Lord. In evaluating prophecy from a particular individual, this discernment is particularly important. Over a period of time it will be possible to get a clear sense of whether a person's prophecy is from the Lord.

There arises within the community (especially among those who are older in its life) a good sense of peace that someone's prophecy is from the Lord, or a clear sense of uneasiness if it is not.

"By their fruits you shall know them" is also an important test of prophecy. When the prophet is responding well to the Lord his words bring forth a good response from the community, conviction of the Lord, and peace with unity about the word.

Sharing

In addition to the word gifts of prophecy, tongues, and interpretation of tongues, sharing from our own insight or experience is another means by which the community manifests the glory of the Lord and builds itself up as the Lord's body. Sharing includes exhortation, teaching, and testimony.

Perhaps the most common form of sharing is *exhortation,* moving people to a deeper commitment or to a particular action. Frequently, as the Holy Spirit works, a person begins to sense what the Lord is saying. Not always is this sense meant to be put into the form of prophecy, but commonly it can be shared as simply a sense of the Lord's word speaking to what we are or must become. It is not a word meant just for our information but for our transformation, and it is natural to communicate it as an exhortation—a calling to heed the Lord and turn in the way he commands.

Such exhortation has a prophetic quality. In the New Testament we sometimes see prophets speaking in this way. After the council of Jerusalem described in Acts 15, Judas and Silas are sent to Antioch to bring news of the council's decision. After reading the decision, the two men continued to speak: *"And Judas and Silas, who were themselves prophets, exhorted the brethren with many words and strengthened them"* (Acts 15:32).

Another common form of sharing at a prayer meeting can generally be described as *teaching.* There is a place in the prayer meeting for more developed or formal teachings, but there are often things shared that serve as teaching. One person may read a passage from Scripture and comment on it to bring out the meaning he feels is intended. Or someone may share an insight into some Christian truth with enough development so that all can understand it. Or someone may share an understanding of how the Lord wants us to live, and in his explanation bring together several texts from Scripture. Such sharing can contain genuine wisdom from the Lord, especially when it proceeds from the Lord's own word in Scripture: *"Let the word of Christ dwell in you richly, as you teach and admonish one another in all wisdom"* (Col. 3:16).

Testimony, another form of sharing in meetings, means simply the sharing from personal experience of the Lord's action in our lives so that others may see the reality and goodness of the Lord and be led to love and praise him more. Testimony may include everything from a detailed account of one's conversion to a simple sharing of a brief event that shows God's action.

Many of us have experienced the power of good testimony: there is no need to convince ourselves of its great value in a meeting, but there is much to learn. How often have we heard testimony that was distracting, rambling, self-centered, and confused? The sharing of testimony to the Lord's action is of such great value that we ought to make the effort to learn how to do it. At the outset, we must remember that sharing is to glorify the Lord and to build up others, not to glorify or focus attention on ourselves. There are two opposite problems that relate to this goal: on the one hand we have those who won't speak or share in a meeting out of a false humility and a fear of drawing attention to themselves, and on the other we have some who share out of a sense of insecurity or pride, and, failing to glorify the Lord, they only succeed in asserting themselves.

To the first group, who are probably the more numerous, we must honestly say that it is not right to "hide our light under a bushel" and, out of fear of our weakness, refuse to tell of the Lord's goodness in our lives. God's manifested love ought to be shared so that his glory may be seen. We do have tendencies to want attention and temptations to pride, so let us admit to the Lord those tendencies and ask him to take care of them, and then determine in our heart that we wish to share for the sake of the Lord. The Lord knows well enough how to handle our weaknesses, and can prevent them from harming our testimony.

On the other hand, those who share out of pride or insecurity tend to speak more about themselves than about the Lord. Generally this shows up in a tendency to speak more about their subjective feeling about what the Lord has done than on the objective situation of their life and the action of the Lord in it. Leaders and other mature members of a group ought to supply such brothers and sisters with correction and help in learning how to share.

It is worth noting that there are different kinds of sharing, and that different things are appropriate at different types of meetings. For example, in a small home prayer group of ten to twenty people who know each other personally, it is appropriate to share the kind of intimate things that one might share among Christian friends. Also, in such groups it is appropriate to share more often or to share regularly about what the Lord is doing in a particular area of our life. However, in a larger public prayer meeting of a hundred or even several hundred, these things are not appropriate. In larger meetings it is important that the sharing be oriented to the whole community gathered and not just to those who know us well. Especially appropriate to these situations is sharing of an evangelistic character, about how we met the Lord or were baptized in the Spirit, or sharing that demonstrates the reality and glory of God for those who are new. Further, in those communities which have special prayer meetings for community members, it is appropriate to share testimony oriented to those already committed to the Lord who understand the significance and subtleties of growth in the Lord.

But wherever we do share testimony, there are some guidelines that always hold.

Our testimony should be concise and to the point. Nothing can deaden a testimony more than rambling and irrelevant detail. When we share we ought to include enough concrete detail so that the testimony is alive and interesting, but we should not burden the testimony with unnecessary detail. Again, one of the frequent failings here is to include too much description of one's own subjective state at every moment being described.

We ought to use normal American English in our testimony. Biblical sounding phrases, even from the current translations, do not really speak to the average American. Jargon can also distract us. We will always have the problem of developing a special language since there is so much special that we have in common. Nonetheless, we ought to make an effort to describe things in ordinary language, rather than relying on jargon terms. It is helpful to imagine yourself talking to a friend who is not baptized in the Spirit and speak in a way that even he would understand.

Sharing ought to be objective and sound. We do not have to strain to "pad" the Lord's work. In fact, exaggeration by pentecostals has offended many sincere people, and we ought to avoid such exaggerations.

Sharing is not a means of discussion. Particularly in larger meetings, discussion ought to be reserved for other times, and we should not use sharing as a way of carrying on a discussion, or worse yet, trying to solve problems and disagreements in the meeting itself. This kind of communication is absolutely needed, but the sharing

31

ought to be seen as fitting into a meeting gathered to praise and worship the Lord.

The prayer meeting is not the place to share about one's psychological problems. It is not possible to really care for someone with psychological problems during the meeting itself, since this usually requires more in depth discussion and more long-term support and prayer. A prayer meeting is not designed to be a therapy group. It would of course be appropriate to say that one is having difficulty with depression or whatever it may be and request prayer. When the prayer is answered or when we experience the Lord working to change us, it is appropriate to share this in a way that is upbuilding and encouraging. But simply to talk at length about how confused or miserable we feel, in a situation where nothing can be directly done about it, is inappropriate. Someone with serious psychological problems should not share at all in a prayer meeting until he is receiving the help he needs and the help is working; otherwise his sharing will be off-centered and not upbuilding.

What can be done on the positive side to improve the sharing at a prayer meeting? First it will make a big difference if the more mature members of the community who are sensitive to what makes a good sharing set the tone and direction of the meeting. We have noticed that in many prayer meetings, the older members of the community are reluctant to share. It seems to be young Christians, newly-baptized in the Spirit, who share most often. But older members ought to take responsibility for the effectiveness of the meeting, and one important way is through sharing. If the more mature members share well, it sets an example for the younger members to share well also.

A second help to having better sharing in the meeting is having a prepared testimony as part of the meeting. The way people learn to share well is through seeing it done well. Many groups have found that having someone prepare in advance to share his testimony in the meeting enables him to do a good job, and at the same time his example, like leaven, raises the quality of sharing in the meeting in general. We usually have one of the leaders ask someone to prepare a testimony for each meeting, and then work with them to teach them how to organize it, to include relevant detail, and to present it well.

A third way we can improve the sharing in our prayer meeting is by giving feedback to those who exhort or testify; encourage them when we feel they have responded well to the Lord, and give them confidence to share in the future. Give them suggestions for improvements, and help them grow in their ability to share. Since one purpose of sharing is to build up the community, a person needs to find out if his sharing did that or not. If someone shares at a meeting and does not receive any feedback, he ought to approach one of the group's leaders and ask for his discernment about the sharing.

Sharing can be a powerful tool of the Lord. We have seen people's lives changed because they heard a testimony that revealed the Lord to them. We know that the Lord receives such sharing as an offering of praise and thanksgiving.

Not without reason did the Holy Spirit inspire the psalmist to exclaim, *"I will tell of thy name to my brethren; in the midst of the congregation I will praise thee"* (Ps. 22:22).

Responding to God's Word

So far we have spoken primarily about the person speaking the word. Let's consider for a moment our response to it. For if we do not respond as the Lord desires we will fail to fully receive his word. In responding we need to hear and consider the word and be obedient to it. It is the word of the Lord that we are dealing with, so we must take it seriously. There are sometimes impediments to hearing the word that we can introduce by not responding well. One common failing is to not allow time for the word to penetrate. Some have a tendency to start a song or prayer as soon as a prophecy is spoken so that we never really have time to consider it. Better to pause in quiet prayer as we consider the word. Or, in some instances, as when the word calls us to praise, we should respond with more fervent prayer.

Another response that is often appropriate is to confirm the message if we have felt the Lord saying the same thing to us. This not only emphasizes the truth of the message, but it can be a great encouragement to the one who prophesied.

"The word of God is living and active, sharper than any two-edged sword, piercing to the division of soul and spirit, of joints and marrow, and discerning the thoughts and intentions of the

heart.'' (Hebrews 4:12). God's word comes to us with a purpose, alive and actively working in our hearts. If we learn to yield to the Lord in speaking his word, and to actively respond to that word, it will bring us new life.

CHAPTER THREE

Order in the Meeting

In the center a group of guitarists begin to play. "Sing to God a brand new, brand new canticle..." When the song ends the prayer meeting leader is already standing in the middle. "Let the nations shout and clap their hands for joy.

Two elements have emerged as significant factors in fostering unity and peace in our Christian gatherings. The first is the development of various types of meetings. The second is the role of the leader in these meetings. In discussing the order in prayer meetings, the patterns of relationships and participation that allow us to pray in unity and peace, it is important to realize the relationship of the order of the meeting to the rest of our Christian lives.

Types of Meetings

Earlier, we mentioned that the type of meeting often dictates the type of sharing. If we fail to understand the significance of different types of prayer meetings, we are likely to encounter two opposite problems. On the one hand, there will be those people who expect too much of the meeting, on the other hand those who do not expect enough. The former may complain of a large prayer meeting, "We just don't have that closeness we had when we were meeting in so-and-so's living room." The latter may be uncomfortable if their large meeting should develop into anything more than a weekly gathering for random personal sharing with minimal leadership.

These problems rise from a misunderstanding of the different types of prayer meeting. The first people are expecting a large prayer group to have the same kind of personal intimacy as a small home meeting, only with more people. What we have learned is that as prayer groups grow in size new kinds of personal relationships are formed. The close friendships possible in a small group are not possible with a hundred people. The desire for and need of these close supportive relationships must be met by smaller groupings within the larger structure.

Among the second group of people, those uncomfortable with developing structure, just the opposite has happened. In a small group, one does not expect (nor necessarily need) a developed leadership group, regular teaching, Life in the Spirit Seminars, or directive (and corrective) prayer meeting leadership. But when a smaller group grows to fifty or more people without developing the kind of leadership and services appropriate to that type of meeting, its meetings will become lifeless and unsatisfying. New people will drift in and out again without receiving the help they need to find the Lord.

When we speak of the different types of prayer meetings, we have five types particularly in mind: 1) introductory meetings, 2) small prayer meetings, 3) large open meetings, 4) core groups, or community meetings, and 5) mass meetings. Each has a certain unique purpose and is characterized by particular kinds of relationships, order, and services.

Introductory meetings are used to introduce charismatic prayer to a group of people who have no knowledge of it. This is the kind of meeting a group of people invited to another city to introduce the charismatic renewal might lead. Or a couple moving from a city where they were involved in a prayer group might invite an interested group of their new neighbors to an introductory meeting in their home.

The introductory meeting requires very directive leadership. Very little can be presumed in the way of personal relationships among the participants, and only the leaders and their assistants will have any idea of what is appropriate to a prayer meeting. Unless clearly directed as to what they can do to participate, the new people will feel that they are merely observers.

Introductory meetings generally begin with an explanation by the leaders covering the charismatic renewal, the baptism of the Spirit, spiritual gifts, and prayer meetings. A few personal testimonies help to make it all real. But what people usually want most is to see for themselves, and so there is the prayer meeting itself. The leader should explain each part of the meeting, tell people what things would be appropriate for them to join in, and periodically explain what has happened (e.g., explaining the significance of prophecy or a message in tongues with interpretation). The experienced helpers in the meeting need to be very supportive and active in prayer, witnessing, and sharing.

We won't say anything further about this type of meeting here, but we mention it because it illustrates how very different the leadership and personal relationships within a prayer meeting can be depending on the type of meeting.

Small prayer groups, gatherings of less than twenty-five people, usually about ten or twelve, meet in homes, or among the residents of a seminary or college dormitory. The group is small enough for everyone to have close personal relationships. People frequently know one another well even before the prayer group begins. If not, close relationships develop quickly.

Because the meeting is a small gathering of close friends, it is usually appropriate for persons to share their lives in an intimate way. They can also respond directly to something another says.

For example, when one person describes a difficulty he has encountered, another may speak up with a word of encouragement or advice, This semi-personal counseling is usually inappropriate at a larger meeting. Sharing at a small meeting should be more active than at a large one, simply because there are fewer people. Because sharing is active, lively, and intimate, small groups are especially effective in supporting individual lives. Even members of large communities need small prayer and fellowship groups for direct personal support and prayer. Most communities meet this need by forming households, or small non-residential or neighborhood groupings that meet regularly.

Leadership in a small prayer group is more informal than in a large meeting. The host of the small meeting may serve as a leader, or the leadership may rotate among the more experienced members. Though everyone can contribute to leading a small meeting, a single leader should be designated. His role is primarily to begin and end the meeting and to deal with any problems that come up. As in all meetings the role of the leader is important, but in small prayer groups the style of the leadership is informal.

The dynamics of a small prayer group are usually more complex than the simple pattern of a large meeting. The large meeting usually opens with a long period of praise and worship at the beginning (perhaps 30 minutes). This period includes a number of songs. Next comes a period of sharing, exhortation and teaching (normally including a prepared teaching). The large meeting ends with announcements and singing. While a small prayer group may also begin with worship and praise, it can develop more quickly and flexibly. For example, the Lord may develop a theme through sharing and prophecy; the participants may be led to another period of worship; another theme may be developed; one person may give a teaching; there may be an opportunity for individual ministry and prayer at the end.

The large open meeting is becoming so common that we might call it the characteristic gathering of the charismatic renewal. These meetings may range in size from 50 to more than a thousand, but in most respects they are quite similar in form.

The personal relationships in such meetings are not all close friendships. We may know most of the people by name, but probably not very personally. But we *are* brothers and sisters in the Lord. We have been baptized in the Spirit and have experienced the Spirit's work. We have heard the same teaching and share a great deal of unity in our basic commitments, even though we have not talked personally in much depth. At large open meetings we aim our sharing at a larger audience than just our friends. Since we seek to build up everyone, we share those aspects of our lives that are most relevant to everyone.

We should generally seek a more direct inspiration from the Spirit for sharing at a larger meeting. A good thought, appropriate for a small meeting, may simply obstruct the Lord's word at a larger meeting. Since there is not enough time for everyone to talk, it is very important that we share those things that the Lord wants everyone to hear. In general we should expect the Lord to speak clearly and directly to a large group. We need to be attentive to what he wants to say, even though our needs and inclinations may differ greatly.

The leaders in a large open meeting have a much more visible important role. Generally, the leader is the only person in the meeting in a good position to maintain the meeting's unity. And if any correction needs to be done, he is the only person who can do it. When others try to provide the primary direction and unity or correct some problem in the meeting, all they usually do is to add one more voice to the situation.

When we ask someone to lead a large meeting, we are giving him a special service—to help us pray in unity. It is essential that we support him. This means not only praying for him and encouraging him, but responding to him during the meeting. If the leader asks us to wait quietly in prayer for a few minutes, he ought to be taken seriously. Someone who immediately starts a song or jumps up to speak after such a direction not only ignores the leader, but introduces disunity and confusion into the meeting. If another brother or sister feels moved to suggest a particular direction for the meeting—that we pray over everyone who is sick, for example—he or she should make that suggestion to the leader, allowing him to move the meeting in that direction or to call upon someone to do so. The larger the meeting, the more important it is to have the leader keep the unity and direction.

It has been our experience that the large open meeting contributes something to our personal lives and to the work of the Lord which small prayer groups cannot. The meeting is not only an inspiration, but an important way in which the Lord can speak to us. In larger prayer meetings there are usually better resources for teaching and prophecy than in a small group, and we can frequently hear the Lord's word more clearly and powerfully. The large meeting can also be a powerful witness to non-Christians and other Christians coming for the first time. There is something about the sight of several hundred people worshipping freely, singing, sharing, and teaching about the Lord which is very impressive and powerful.

"Core group" or community meetings have been developing throughout the country, usually after a large open meeting has developed. These are not public meetings. They are not publicized and newcomers are not invited to come. Nor are they particularly evangelistic; the participants already share a basic commitment to the Lord. Core or community meetings are for those who are already baptized in the Spirit and who are committed to one another. In these meetings the Lord can speak more directly to the needs of a more committed group: how can we be a committed community, how should we share the Gospel with others? The dynamics and leadership of these meetings are very similar to those of the large open meeting, but is is important to note the special character of this type of meeting.

"Mass meetings" are very large gatherings such as we have experienced at conferences and at

days of renewal. Mass meetings require very directive leadership. They also require a special approach to the spiritual gifts. In order to be heard, those who prophesy must speak into a microphone. They should be seated near the microphone and they must know when it is appropriate to speak in prophecy. Because of the large numbers, it is crucial that the Lord's word come clearly. At mass meetings, the leaders usually request that only a group of mature and tested prophets prophesy. This does not mean that others cannot hear the word of the Lord. In fact, many people usually will know the message. The point is that only sensitive and experienced prophets should speak the message if everyone is to hear it clearly. If too many people try to speak the word, confusion results.

Our participation in a mass meeting is vital even if we know we will not share or prophesy or teach. If we are not intent upon seeking the Lord we shall hinder the Spirit and be like a dead weight upon the meeting. We ought to participate in worship, singing, and prayer with the same expectant faith as we would in our own prayer group.

The order for mass meetings can vary. For example, we may permit anyone to prophesy but also ask a group of experienced and mature prophets to pray together before the meeting and take a special concern for speaking the Lord's word clearly. We may allow anyone to speak. Or we may ask those who wish to speak to first talk to one of the leaders whose service is to discern what the Lord wants spoken. Whatever the particular order, we know that the Lord wants to work very powerfully at a mass meeting. When we go to such a meeting, we ought to expect our experience to be different than in our prayer group. We ought to see the greater order and structure not as an obstacle to the Spirit, but rather as a tool to facilitate his free working—even among thousands.

Leadership in Prayer Meetings

Almost all of us in the charismatic renewal have had some bad experiences with prayer meetings that suffered from a lack of order. Sometimes the problem showed up in the deadness of the meeting because of lack of direction. Other times the problem showed up in lack of coherence: everything going in different directions in a random, scattered way that left everyone feeling tense and confused. At times the meeting would get off into tangents, be deluged with strange sharings, or drift aimlessly.

We have also experienced extraordinarily good meetings because of proper order. We have seen small groups and even great crowds at international conferences move in unity and peace in a prayer meeting. Where there has been good order, we have had the feeling that we could stop worrying about what would happen next, and be free to pray and seek the Lord. Order makes a big difference.

Order in a prayer meeting begins with the leader. In fact, the very acceptance of a prayer meeting leader is an act of establishing some order to the meeting. When we first began to have prayer meetings, they tended to be leaderless. While it worked well for a small group, as soon as there were more than a few friends praying together, it created problems. Because there was no leader, we did not even have a method for ending the prayer meeting. They often lasted about five hours; they ended because they had to.

Having no leader in a prayer meeting that was growing in size was edging us towards chaos. The meetings were becoming more confused. The word of the Lord was not being spoken clearly, and disruptions were possible at anytime by anybody. Our sense of peace in the Lord was being lost. Therefore, the first element of order was added—someone to lead the meeting.

It was not the job of the leader to "run" the meeting, but to provide unity and direction for the meeting and to have the authority to handle problems that came up in the meeting. In addition, the leader served the meeting by setting a good direction at the beginning and periodically exhorting us to seek the Lord or to listen or share or sing.

The agreement to have and accept a leader is done for the sake of being able to move in unity. It does not imply that the leader will always do exactly the right thing. Indeed, he is bound to make mistakes. But when we might all have a different idea of what to do next in a prayer meeting, and yet wish to do something together in unity, the leader can give us a direction which we have agreed to accept in order to have unity.

St. Paul exhorts us in 1 Corinthians 14 to "make love your aim." Our goal is to make love and unity the characteristic of the meeting—not to win a dispute over what is the right course of action during a meeting.

A prayer meeting leader needs to experience our support and encouragement. We must respond to his leading. We should also encourage him in his work and give him feedback that will help him to grow in his service and benefit from successes and mistakes.

While order in a prayer meeting is facilitated by having a leader, and agreeing to submit to that leader, another type of order develops as patterns grow up in the meeting. For example, we learned very early that it was a great help to begin the meeting with a substantial period of time given to worship and prayer and song. This has become an expected pattern in our meetings, so that little needs to be said about it. One might say the meeting is ordered by this pattern: the first part of the meeting is reserved to prayer and worship, and the latter part of the meeting is open to testimony, teaching, etc. This means that during the first part of the meeting all can be free to pray or speak the word of the Lord in prophecy, and each knows that he or she is supported by the whole community in this direction. The first part of the meeting can move with unity, since everyone is expecting to pray in a particular way.

Another example of order in a prayer meeting is the pattern of our response to a prophecy or a message in tongues. When there is a message in tongues we know that the appropriate thing to do is wait for the interpretation. But, through teaching by the leader, it can also become part of the pattern of our meetings that after a prophecy or interpretation we consider the word of the Lord and respond to it in some way other than immediately jumping into a song, sharing, or a further word of the Lord.

Leading the singing at a prayer meeting is another important pastoral responsibility. The song leader often affects the spirit and direction of the prayer meeting more than anyone else. Therefore, the song leader should be someone whom the Lord has formed and equipped to serve in this way. There is no reason why most prayer meeting leaders cannot also lead the singing. Even if they do not play an instrument or sing very well, they can have the leading guitarist sit next to them and begin songs when they request them. The same arrangement is appropriate even when there is a song leader. The song leader can sit next to the prayer meeting leader so that both can cooperate in leading the music of the meeting. Probably the most common pattern is to have the song leader, and a group of musicians working together under his leadership, begin some songs, especially at the beginning and end of the meeting, and the prayer meeting leader begin some songs. The prayer meeting leader will also select other songs for the song leader and musicians to introduce. One thing that groups have been learning is that not everyone who can play the guitar is called to be a song leader. Rather, the role of song leader depends upon the ability to sense what the Lord is doing in the meeting and to choose the correct songs to respond to it.

The Prayer Meeting's Relationship to Christian Life

For our prayer meetings to succeed, there is a need for a common understanding of what we are attempting to do. For example, when prayer meetings first began, many took them to be the same thing as a therapy group or a "rap session." Participating in a way that sidetracked the meeting from its purpose, they launched into a discussion on an unrelated topic, or they used the meeting as a place to share all their problems and seek counselling. The problem is larger than this example, of course, and it leads us into the second aspect of order.

A prayer meeting can do certain things in the life of a Christian and of a Christian community, but it cannot be expected to do everything. Expecting too much from a prayer meeting can overburden it and prevent it from doing what God intends it to do. A prayer meeting cannot solve psychological problems. Deep problems need to be dealt with, and the Lord wants to heal them, but they can only be dealt with in a situation different from the prayer meeting. Perhaps what will be needed is personal counselling, or a special group. A prayer meeting is not a friendship group, especially prayer meetings larger than ten or twelve. We cannot expect the prayer meeting to form all our deep relationships, which we do need and ought to have. We must expect that it is not possible to be close friends with everyone in a big prayer meeting. Rather, the life of the group beyond the prayer meeting ought to provide other ways of developing friendships. When people mistakenly expect the prayer meeting to satisfy all of their needs for personal friendship, they often feel frustrated and tend to put pressure on the group to be more than it ought to be.

A related problem shows itself in those who expect the prayer meeting to be a place to share all their thoughts or everything about their lives. There is not time enough for this, nor is there opportunity for response. There is need for opportunities outside the prayer meeting for the kind of sharing and fellowship each person needs. Further, the prayer meeting is not able to meet all a person's needs for prayer. Each person also needs time for personal prayer in addition to the group prayer of the meeting. Trying to use the prayer meeting to satisfy the needs for personal prayer detracts from the united worship of the whole group.

Discussions are very much needed for our growth as Christians, too—discussions about Christian living, the Scriptures, problems we encounter, etc. But discussions are "out of order" at a prayer meeting. When we feel the need for more discussion among our prayer group members, we ought to recognize that the solution is probably outside the scope of the meeting itself. We also learned early that it was not appropriate to make the prayer meeting the place to prepare people to be baptized in the Spirit. The Life in the Spirit Seminars were developed for use outside the actual prayer meeting to meet the need for this kind of instruction.

The prayer meeting is a place where God's love comes alive, and where God can work to form us into his people. But the meeting cannot do everything needed in building up a body of Christians. It has a definite and important role, but it must be supplemented by other things if it is to function effectively to build up the body of Christ.

We mentioned the pressure that people sometimes place on the prayer meeting, expecting it to answer all the needs of their Christian life. The meeting cannot do this because the Christian life consists of more than just going to meetings. But the meeting should be an accurate reflection of the Christian life. The spiritual gifts, the prayer, the songs are all aspects of our daily life, the life of the body the Holy Spirit is forming. The order, the sharings and yielding to the spiritual gifts, are acts of service to our brothers and sisters, reflecting the service that should characterize the daily life of a Christian.

CHAPTER FOUR

Evangelism at Prayer Meetings

As people enter the high school gymnasium, a smiling girl distributing name tags pauses to greet one man who obviously feels out of place. They spend a few minutes talking before he rejoins the crowd.

Not too long ago we received a letter that contained an all-too-common story of a man who attended his first prayer meeting and met such indifference he almost never returned. Getting out of his car in the parking lot of an average midwestern church, he asked directions to the location of the prayer meeting. Several people indicated the direction, but no one spoke to him or invited him to go with them. When he entered the parish hall he found the twenty-five "regulars" in vigorous conversation and the eight "newcomers" standing around talking to no one. His efforts to speak to some regulars drew a cool "hello." When the meeting ended the newcomers were directed to a corner of the room to meet with one of the regulars. Dutifully they gathered, but no one came. Everyone else was busy talking and having refreshments. The eight visitors were the last to leave.

Sad or comical as this story may seem, it actually happened. It dramatizes the problem of greeting those who come to our prayer meetings for the first time. Almost every prayer group can think of one or two instances in which their own prayer group seriously offended some interested person who came to their meeting and met indifference, insensitivity, or rejection. Fortunately, some of the simple solutions are well within the reach of any group willing to invest in the effort of loving those whom the Lord leads to their meeting.

"If you love those who love you, what credit is that to you? For even sinners love those who love them" (Luke 6:32). These words of Jesus are meant for us when we find ourselves in that familiar situation of conflict between talking with our friends or with new visitors to our meetings. It is natural that before and after the prayer meeting we should want to talk to our brothers and sisters. There ought to be such love among Christians: it is a witness to the Lord. Yet, if we

53

greet only our friends "what credit is that to us, even sinners do the same." We should also be aware of the person who has just come for the first time and is standing around wondering what to do next. We should reach out to meet these people, introduce them to others, perhaps ask them how they came to the meeting or explain to them what will be happening so they will be able to be more relaxed. It is not difficult to welcome such a person and include him naturally in our conversation without embarrassing him with too much attention.

We ought to have times when we can talk with the members of our community and build those relationships of love and trust. If our prayer meeting is public, however, we must also be prepared to welcome in love everyone whom the Lord brings. Our great mission is to preach the Gospel to all nations. What better place to start than with those who come to our own prayer meetings? The important need that we have for fellowship should not exclude such an outreach. A wider variety of means can be developed to build and nourish that fellowship.

An opposite problem is focusing excessive attention upon new people present in a meeting so that they feel uncomfortable and put on the spot. I recall one prayer meeting I visited several years ago that had a practice of interrupting the prayer meeting after the first half hour to ask all the new visitors to stand up and introduce themselves. They were then asked to follow one of the leaders to another room where the baptism of the Spirit was explained to them. As they left the room everyone applauded and upon their return all joined in a chorus of "We love you new people, O yes we do. . ." Some were surely delighted at this gesture, but many others were undoubtedly embarrassed. For some it had been all they could do to work up the nerve to come to a meeting in the first place, much less being publically applauded. The group later discontinued this practice, but it demonstrates the error of overenthusiasm in welcoming newcomers. We ought to greet them warmly, talk with them, include them naturally, and give them a chance to see for themselves, trusting the Holy Spirit to work in them.

Not talking to visitors to a prayer meeting communicates an "in" group attitude, but the same attitude can be communicated by what we say. One letter we received came from a priest who had been a missionary for twelve years with great sacrifice and lived as committed and dedicated a Christian life as anyone we have known. Imagine his feelings upon attending his first prayer meeting when a man, recently baptized in the Spirit, virtually discounted his Christianity upon learning that he was not yet baptized in the Spirit: "Oh, so you're not *in* yet." This priest continued to go to prayer meetings anyway, but many of us could relate stories of others who did not return.

In welcoming other Christians to our prayer meetings we should communicate love and acceptance. Our attitude should be that we are all children of God whom God wishes to fill with his Spirit more and more. We can share about our experience of the Holy Spirit in a way that says, "The Lord is doing tremendous things to renew and deepen the life of Christians. We are learning that there is more that he wants to do for us than we have often expected." We can share what he has been doing in us and in our group rather than forcing it upon them. We can also be genuinely interested in another's Christian experience without feeling or communicating that without the baptism in the Spirit it is not worth much. The same Spirit has been at work within them and may now have another step for them.

Sometimes, "in" group impressions are created because prayer group members feel defensive about their experience and want to emphasize that it is real and important. This can be especially true when talking to clergy. We can, with the help of the Lord, free ourselves from such defensiveness. We should trust that the Lord will speak to another person, answer his questions, demonstrate to him the reality of the Holy Spirit. We can witness truthfully and humbly to what God has done for us, keeping in mind that the same God can speak to them also. We can rely on his power and not have to feel that it is up to us to make people believe that the charismatic renewal is genuine. If a person has come to our prayer meeting, it indicates at least some interest and openness, and the Lord who brought him will continue to work in him through the meeting.

Another question in greeting new visitors at our meetings is the problem of what to do when we do greet them. Two particular difficulties come to mind: finding the new people (especially in larger prayer meetings), and giving them adequate explanations and help.

Finding out who the new people are at a larger prayer meeting can be difficult. We discovered this several years ago when we decided to organize a team of "greeters" who would make it their special service to meet the newcomers at the meeting, talk with them, introduce them to others, and help them find the explanation sessions. After a few weeks of effort the new "greeters" shared their experiences. To our chagrin, the majority of the people they had approached as "new" had been coming for months, even years, and frequently were already baptized in the Spirit. But as the group continued to serve, they quickly became familiar with the crowd at the meeting and soon had little difficulty noticing a new face. We have continued the prayer meeting greeters for several years, and it has worked very well. Others in the community are urged to reach out to new people also but the prayer meeting greeters consciously keep track of newcomers and help them to get to know others and find answers to their questions. The greeters welcome the new person, explain a little about the community and the meeting, tell them about the explanation session and Life in the Spirit Seminars, and generally try to help the person feel at home. These greeters do not wear any special designation or identify themselves as "greeters." They simply serve as brothers and sisters with a special concern for visitors. They meet together regularly to share how things are going and to support one another in this service.

Giving adequate explanations and answers to questions is sometimes more than many of the members of the prayer group are capable of. And so most groups make use of a special "explanation (or introductory) session" before or after the prayer meeting. Here a few people of greater experience can present the understanding of the gospel that motivates the prayer group and especially the elements of the charismatic renewal that are generally unfamiliar to new people. Such an explanation session is a good place for people to ask their questions and receive good answers from leaders of the prayer group. Although these sessions are generally called "explanation" or "introductory" sessions, they ought to be seen as occasions to witness to the Gospel. The prayer meetings exist because men and women have believed the Gospel of the Lord and acted upon it. No explanation that leaves out a simple presentation of the Gospel and an invitation to come to the Lord and be filled with his Spirit is complete. Many groups find that having one or two people share brief personal testimonies at such sessions helps people see the reality of the Lord and his Spirit.

These explanation sessions ought to be presented seriously and with appreciation for the great difference they can make in people's lives. Remember that these sessions are probably their first exposure to the charismatic renewal, and for some, perhaps their first exposure to Christianity. An explanation session that is prayerfully well done can very literally change the lives of many people.

The Lord's love impels us to care about every person the Lord leads to our meeting. Loving them and sharing with them the great message the Lord has shared with us is the concrete expression of our mission.

Conclusion

In 2 Chronicles 5, the dramatic story of the dedication of the temple under Solomon is related. From the time that Yahweh gave Moses the plan for the temporary tabernacle erected in the desert, the Israelites had looked forward to the day when the permanent temple of the Lord would be erected in the promised land. And now the building, begun by David and completed years later by Solomon, was finished, and the entire people gathered in Jerusalem for the solemn dedication. The hundreds of priests and Levites took their places, and the hundreds of singers and musicians began to sing and play. And it says that when they lifted their voices, united in giving praise and glory to God, the power of the Lord came so strongly upon the people that the priest fell prostrate upon the temple floor. The entire ceremony came to a halt, for the glory of the Lord filled the house of God.

God reveals himself most powerfully when his people are united in praise and worship: the Lord inhabits the praises of his people (Ps. 22:3). While we may not always be knocked off our feet, as the priests in the temple were, we can expect that when we gather together to worship the Lord he will be among us in glory and power.

The Lord has given us his own Spirit to draw our hearts into his worship. It is the Spirit who inspires and forms our prayer, shaping from our many voices a single, united voice of praise. It is he who speaks God's word through us in prophecy and sharing. It is he who directs our meetings, working through those appointed to lead us. Our part is to become more and more sensitive to his voice as he guides and shapes us in prayer.

The guidelines presented in this book are only effective when our hearts are set upon the Lord and open to the work of his Spirit. As we draw together in his unity, the glory of the Lord will be revealed in our midst.